My Encounter with Bigfoot
(Washington State)

Written By
J.P. Riley

Terms and Legal Notices

The Names, characters, places and incidents mentioned in this book, are the product of the author's memory of actual accounts and experiences to the best of his knowledge.

All of the information and opinions expressed in this book are subject to change over time as science advances.

TABLE OF CONTENTS

CHAPTER 1
SEEING IS BELIEVING

I had just gotten out of the Marines, when my best friend called me up and asked if I'd like to go bow hunting with him. It was late in November and I didn't want to see him go up there alone so I decided to tag along. After a long drive through the snow covered mountains, we finally arrived at a place called The Nile. It's a Game Management Unit located in

Eastern Washington. From there, we turned off onto the 1500 road.

As we made our way up the snow covered road, we both had to stop and chain up due to the icy conditions. I remember noticing how amazing the stars looked once the clouds disappeared but the road started to ice over and it started to get extremely cold, very fast! We drove up the road as far as we could before my truck got stuck in the snow. It was getting late so we decided to set up camp for the night and we quickly got a small fire going. The moon was so bright that it lit up the forest like a spotlight. It was extremely cold out so I decided to throw on my insulated coveralls to keep warm. I walked over to the passenger side of my truck to grab something and out of the corner of my eye, I saw a figure that looked like a tall man, walking up the middle of the road! He was about 15 yards away from where I was parked. I wasn't sure where this guy came from or why was he walking up the road without a flashlight at one thirty in the morning but something just didn't add up!

As he walked closer to me, I couldn't help but notice how tall he was. We didn't see any other hunters when we drove in and we didn't hear one vehicle drive up the road either. As far as I could tell, my friend and I were the only people there at that time. I stood there and watched as the creature got closer and closer to me. I couldn't believe how tall it was. This thing was very dark and it had to be at least 8 to 9 feet tall! It's head and shoulders appeared to be very muscular in size. I also couldn't help but notice its over pronounced arm swing and large gate, as we watched this creature walked effortlessly through 4 feet of snow like it was nothing! We stood there motionless as he got closer to me, I turned to my friend and told him to look. We both watched in shock as this creature walked past us! When the creature got directly in front of me, he turned his head, looked right at me for a brief second and then looked away before disappearing into the forest. I never believed in Bigfoot before that night and I was very much a sceptic until then. I'll never forget what we both saw walking by our camp! I've been bow hunting many times since I was a kid and I know what bears, humans and other wild animals of the forest look like. I know for a fact, that what we saw that night wasn't a bear and it wasn't a human either. We didn't go chasing after it and to this day, I'm not exactly sure why! I spoke to a long time Bigfoot field researcher about the incident and he told me that the Native Americans were afraid to go up onto Bethel Ridge and to this day will not go up there because of Sasquatch! Most people are unaware that they are even in that part of eastern Washington but I know for a fact that they are!

CHAPTER 2
WHAT DID I JUST SEE

Someone once told me that some of the Native Americans believe that Sasquatch has the power to somehow hypnotize people, making them forget what they saw. I'm not sure if that's true or not but that leads me to think that it might have something do with infra sound. Some people believe that Bigfoot uses infra sound to communicate, just like elephants and dolphins do. This is a sound that resonates on a different frequency than our human ears can hear. It's known to affect our senses in a strange way, which could possibly explain why we didn't go chasing after it. When you see something that large in the wilderness, it's kind of like seeing a grizzly bear walk by you at 15 yards away and you probably wouldn't want to go chasing after that either. The ancient Greeks believed that a lynx

could see through solid objects and

science has taught us that dogs and

other wild animals can sense fear in

other creatures as well. There are many

different types of creatures living on

this planet that all possess unique

abilities and talents. Many of these

abilities started off as myths that were

later proven by science to be actual

facts. I know what I saw up there that

night but I believe without a doubt that

there's an unidentified North American

Primate living and breathing in the

Pacific Northwest!

CHAPTER 3
WHY SO LITTLE EVIDENCE

Why don't a lot of people including hunters see Bigfoot more often and why don't they get any good pictures of them? Here's my theory. Most avid hikers, campers and hunters, do most of their hiking during the daylight hours when they can see the best, without having to use artificial light. Most of them don't go too far off of the main trails and most don't go more than three quarters of a mile from their vehicles. The ones that do generally

don't do it at night, especially in remote

parts of the wilderness where there aren't

any trails. Sadly enough, a lot of hunters

don't even get out of their trucks! So what

does that leave us with? It leaves us with

sounds. Over the years a handful of people

recorded different sounds and

vocalizations. Scientists then used

computerized software to analyze those

sounds and based on their findings they

concluded that the vocalizations came from

the diaphragm of a large, unidentified

primate! A lot of these sounds were

recorded in the remote parts of the Pacific

Northwest by people who are legit and not

considered to be flaky or mentally unstable

in any way. It's very interesting if you

think about it. Our world is full of

unexplainable things that go bump in the

night. Is it all just a figment of our

imagination or could there be something

concrete behind all of these claims? Will

there ever be enough evidence to prove

beyond a reasonable doubt that Bigfoot does indeed exist or will this elusive primate remain a mystery throughout time? As our population keeps growing and more forests disappear to make room for cities Sasquatch may end up being nothing more than a myth to modern day science. I believe that it will take hard work and a lot of exploring to uncover one of the Pacific Northwest's most unravelling mystery! Time is by no means on our side!

CHAPTER 4
FINDINGS AND FACTS

Scientists are now using state of the art forensic technology to analyze some of the evidence that's been found in various locations around the world. Despite recent findings, a lot of people still fail to believe that there's an unidentified North American Primate that lives in the Pacific Northwest. Ironically enough, the justice system has convicted people for murder based on less evidence than what we have found to support the evidence of Bigfoot's existence. There are handfuls of collections of many different types of tracks that have been documented and analyzed throughout the years that are believed to be from an unknown North American Primate! These casts have clear dermal ridge patterns on them and other important features. Strangely enough, the technology and instruments for measuring dermal ridge patterns didn't even exist back when some of the tracks were casted and if it did, the early technology wasn't nearly as advanced as it is today. I don't even think we knew about dermal ridge patterns back then, let alone the scientific data to test the validity of them either. The technology just wasn't around at the time to fabricate that kind of evidence. Evidence like that really can't fool modern day science! Even today, it would be extremely hard for someone to pull off a hoax of that nature because of how good our forensic scientists are at finding facts from fiction.

Most people have no clue as to what goes into a footprint or a set of them. Each time a person takes a step there are millions of things happening such as pressure ridges, dermal ridges, the gate, the animal's weight and a bunch of other scientific clues. There are experts out there who have masters degrees in Forensic Anthropology that have studied these footprints for many years. They believe without a shadow of a doubt that there's an unknown North American primate that lives in a few isolated places of North America! Despite all of the sightings and evidence that we do have there's been a lot of hoaxers who go out of their way to fake evidence. I feel that because of this, the scientific community has lost a lot of motivation to put any real effort into finding this elusive primate! Many scientists are worried that their image will be tarnished if they get caught trying to prove the existence of Bigfoot!

CHAPTER 5
SUMMING IT ALL UP

Based on my beliefs, I believe that the Sasquatch around Bethel Ridge stay up as high as they can to avoid humans and then migrate down to the lowlands in the fall to graze like the elk on wild edibles. I also believe that the snow pushes them down to lower elevations. In some places throughout the Pacific Northwest, the large bull elk will stay up as high as possible until the snow gets deep enough to drive them down. I think that A Sasquatch only comes down as far as the snow level pushes them and then they sort of migrate with the snow level depending on their environment and terrain. I've also heard that on average, scientists discover at least one new primate a year that we didn't know existed. Will we ever have concrete proof of the existence of a North American Great Ape or will this unexplained phenomenon remain a mystery in time?

I'd like to thank everyone for taking the time to read my books. It's been a long journey which has spanned over two years and I couldn't have wrote this book without your support. Best of Luck in your Bigfoot Adventures.

Thanks again!

J.P. Riley